MAYER SMITH

A Dance with the Silver-Eyed Sorcerer

Copyright © 2025 by Mayer Smith

All rights reserved. No part of this publication may be reproduced, stored or transmitted in any form or by any means, electronic, mechanical, photocopying, recording, scanning, or otherwise without written permission from the publisher. It is illegal to copy this book, post it to a website, or distribute it by any other means without permission.

This novel is entirely a work of fiction. The names, characters and incidents portrayed in it are the work of the author's imagination. Any resemblance to actual persons, living or dead, events or localities is entirely coincidental.

Mayer Smith asserts the moral right to be identified as the author of this work.

Mayer Smith has no responsibility for the persistence or accuracy of URLs for external or third-party Internet Websites referred to in this publication and does not guarantee that any content on such Websites is, or will remain, accurate or appropriate.

Designations used by companies to distinguish their products are often claimed as trademarks. All brand names and product names used in this book and on its cover are trade names, service marks, trademarks and registered trademarks of their respective owners. The publishers and the book are not associated with any product or vendor mentioned in this book. None of the companies referenced within the book have endorsed the book.

First edition

*This book was professionally typeset on Reedsy.
Find out more at reedsy.com*

Contents

1	The Moonlit Encounter	1
2	Whispers of the Past	8
3	A Dangerous Invitation	15
4	The Sorcerer's Curse	22
5	A Pact with Darkness	29
6	The Dance of Shadows	36
7	The Silver-Eyed Secret	42
8	Unraveling Threads	49
9	The Silver Blade	56
10	Temptation's Edge	62
11	A Heart Torn Asunder	68
12	The Betrayal	74
13	The Heart of the Curse	80
14	The Final Dance	86
15	The Price of Freedom	92

One

The Moonlit Encounter

The wind whispered through the trees, an ancient language that Mira could almost understand if she let herself listen closely enough. The scent of damp earth and blooming nightshade filled the air as she trekked deeper into the Enchanted Forest. The moon hung high above, casting an ethereal glow that turned the world into a place of secrets and shadows. Every step she took seemed to echo in the stillness, though she was certain no one else was near.

But she was wrong.

Mira's heart skipped a beat as she heard a faint rustle behind her. The wind? A branch snapping? She spun around, breath catching in her throat, but the forest seemed unchanged. The same towering trees, their limbs twisting like fingers reaching for the sky, their leaves shimmering with a silvery sheen. Yet, something was wrong. Something she couldn't place.

Her pulse quickened. It was as if the very air around her thickened, pressing down, urging her to run.

Mira hesitated, her instincts warring with her rational mind. She had ventured into the forest before, countless times, drawn to its mysteries. But tonight, it felt different. The silence felt heavy, suffocating. There was a tension in the air that made her skin prickle, like a storm was about to break.

Then, she saw him.

He stood between two ancient oaks, partially hidden by their dark trunks, his silhouette outlined by the pale moonlight. Tall, with broad shoulders, he appeared as though he had materialized from the shadows themselves. His hair was dark as night, falling in wild waves around his face. But it was his eyes that caught her attention—silver eyes, glowing faintly in the darkness. They weren't the usual eyes of a man. No, these eyes were ancient, and they seemed to see through her, to pierce into her very soul.

Her breath caught in her throat. For a moment, Mira couldn't move, caught in the trance of his gaze. There was a pull, a magnetic force drawing her toward him, and despite the fear tightening in her chest, she found herself stepping forward.

"Who are you?" she whispered, her voice trembling despite her attempt to sound steady.

The Moonlit Encounter

The man didn't answer. He didn't even blink. Instead, he took a step toward her, his movements fluid, almost predatory. Mira instinctively took a step back, the hairs on the back of her neck standing on end.

"I'm not here to hurt you," his voice was low, smooth like velvet, but there was an edge to it—an intensity that made the forest feel colder.

Mira's heartbeat raced as he closed the distance between them. He was close now, so close she could see the faint scars etched into his skin, the shadows under his eyes, and the strange, almost unnatural glow of his silver gaze. It was as if the moonlight clung to him, casting an otherworldly aura around his figure.

"What do you want from me?" Mira demanded, trying to muster some courage, though her throat felt dry. She had heard of him—the Silver-Eyed Sorcerer. The one who haunted the deepest parts of the Enchanted Forest, the one whose power was said to be as old as the earth itself. The stories were always told in hushed whispers, and she never believed them. Not until now.

"I need your help," he finally spoke, his words measured, as if weighing their importance. "I've been waiting for you."

Mira blinked, a flicker of confusion clouding her mind. "Waiting for me? Why?"

His lips curled into a faint smile, one that didn't quite reach his eyes. "You're the one who can break the curse."

Her breath hitched. "The curse?"

"Yes," he said, stepping even closer, and Mira's pulse spiked. She wanted to run, to flee from the terror building in her chest, but her feet remained rooted to the spot. "The curse that binds me."

Before she could respond, a loud crack sounded from behind them. Mira spun around, her heart hammering in her chest. The trees shook, their branches rattling violently as if the forest itself were coming alive.

And then, the shadows gathered.

Dark, serpentine shapes slithered between the trunks of the trees, their movements swift and ominous. They were creatures—some she couldn't even comprehend, their forms shifting in and out of view, like nightmares given flesh. Their eyes glowed red, and the air seemed to grow colder still as they circled them, their intent clear.

Kaleb—he must have sensed her fear because in an instant, his hand was on her arm, pulling her closer. The warmth of his touch was grounding, but there was an undeniable power behind it. Mira could feel the surge of energy, ancient and wild, running through his veins, a force that was both exhilarating and terrifying.

"They won't stop," Kaleb muttered, his silver eyes flashing with an intensity that sent a shiver down her spine. "You need to trust me."

Mira wanted to scream, to demand answers, but her voice failed her. The creatures drew closer, their hissing voices rising in unison, their hunger palpable. Kaleb's grip tightened on her arm as he whispered something in an ancient language, words she couldn't understand. The air crackled with power, and for a moment, everything stilled.

Then, the shadows lunged.

Kaleb's hand shot up, and a burst of blinding light erupted from his palm. It wasn't like anything Mira had ever seen before—pure magic, raw and untamed, swirling in a vortex of power. The creatures recoiled, hissing in fury as the light pushed them back.

But there were too many. Mira could hear their snarls, feel their claws scraping against the earth, closing in on them. Her heart raced, her body trembling as she realized the true danger she was in.

"We're not safe here," Kaleb said urgently, his voice no longer calm, but filled with an edge of desperation. He pulled her toward him, his strength overwhelming as he dragged her through the thick underbrush.

They ran.

Mira's breath came in short gasps as they sprinted through the forest, the creatures' pursuit relentless. The ground beneath her feet seemed to shift, the trees blurring as they sped past. Kaleb's presence beside her was both a comfort and a warning. His power crackled in the air around them, but even he couldn't hold the shadows at bay forever.

"Who are they?" Mira gasped, her voice shaky. "What do they want with us?"

"Those are the shadow creatures of the cursed realm," Kaleb replied, his voice strained. "They're after me—and you. We need to reach the clearing, where the barrier is strong enough to keep them out."

Mira's head spun. What was happening? The man with the silver eyes, the creatures from the depths of nightmare, the curse that seemed to bind them all together—she couldn't make sense of it.

And yet, despite everything, her heart was pounding with an almost irrational need to trust him.

They reached the clearing, the trees opening up to reveal a circle of ancient stones, glowing faintly with a strange blue light. Kaleb pushed her into the center of the circle and raised his hand toward the sky. The wind howled, the air crackling with energy, and for a moment, everything went still.

The shadows stopped at the edge of the clearing, hissing in frustration, unable to cross the boundary Kaleb had drawn. Mira's chest heaved as she caught her breath, her heart racing from the terror they had just escaped.

But it wasn't over. Not yet.

Kaleb turned to her, his eyes intense, his voice low and filled with urgency.

"You have to listen to me, Mira. This isn't just about the curse. There's something far worse coming."

She didn't know what to say, her mind reeling from everything that had just happened. But one thing was certain—nothing in her life would ever be the same again.

And that was just the beginning.

Two

Whispers of the Past

The night air clung to Mira's skin as she made her way back to the village. Her boots crushed the dry leaves beneath her, the sound eerily loud in the silence of the forest. She could still feel the tremors of what had happened in the clearing—Kaleb's touch on her arm, the raw, untamed power that had pulsed between them. His silver eyes, glowing with secrets and sorrow, haunted her thoughts.

She couldn't shake the image of the creatures, those shadowy monstrosities that had pursued them with such ferocity. They were no mere nightmares, but tangible threats that had almost torn them apart. And yet, amidst the chaos, there had been Kaleb—unflinching, powerful, and otherworldly. His power had saved them, but it also left her with more questions than answers.

Her feet seemed to carry her of their own accord, her mind racing with everything she had just witnessed. It was hard to believe it had been only hours since she'd stumbled into the forest, unaware of the dangers lurking within. Now, as she neared the village, Mira's chest tightened with uncertainty. What would she say to her family? To her grandmother?

"Mira!" A voice cut through the thick air, startling her. She spun around to see Lyanna, the village healer, stepping from the shadows of the trees. Lyanna's sharp eyes gleamed with suspicion, her expression unreadable.

Mira exhaled sharply, her heart still racing. "Lyanna," she said, forcing the word out through dry lips. She had no idea what to say, no way to explain the strange encounter in the forest. How could she? She could hardly believe it herself.

"You've been gone longer than usual." Lyanna's gaze swept over her, lingering on her disheveled appearance. Mira felt the heat rise to her cheeks, though she couldn't explain why. There was no shame in running through the woods, not when she had been chased by monsters. Still, something about Lyanna's piercing eyes made her feel small.

"I... I lost track of time," Mira said, but the words felt hollow.

Lyanna's eyes narrowed, sensing the lie, but she didn't press the issue. "You should be careful, Mira. The forest is dangerous at night."

Mira didn't reply, her mind still tangled in thoughts of Kaleb.

Of his eyes, glowing like twin moons in the dark. Of the curse he had mentioned. And of the shadows that had followed them.

"I'm fine," Mira said, brushing past her, eager to return to the comfort of her grandmother's cottage. But Lyanna's next words stopped her in her tracks.

"Don't trust him, Mira."

Mira's heart thudded painfully in her chest, and she spun back around. "What do you mean?"

Lyanna's face was shadowed, her expression unreadable. "The Silver-Eyed Sorcerer," she said, her voice low and filled with warning. "He's not what he seems. There are stories about him, Mira. Dark stories."

A shiver ran down Mira's spine. "I don't understand."

"You will," Lyanna said softly, her gaze flicking to the trees behind them. "You'll learn soon enough."

Before Mira could ask another question, Lyanna turned and disappeared into the night, her footsteps fading into the distance. Mira stood there for a moment, the weight of her words sinking in. The Silver-Eyed Sorcerer. That was what they called Kaleb. The name sounded like a curse, like something to be feared, and yet… there had been something in his touch, something that had felt both dangerous and irresistible.

The village appeared ahead of her, nestled on the edge of the forest, its stone cottages glowing with warm, golden light. Mira's heart felt heavy as she entered the small community, the familiar sights of her home doing little to calm the unease that simmered within her.

She found her grandmother in the kitchen, stirring a pot of herbs. The faint scent of lavender filled the room, mingling with the smell of firewood crackling in the hearth.

"Grandmother," Mira said softly, her voice thick with emotion.

Her grandmother looked up from her task, her wise old eyes meeting Mira's with a knowing gaze. "You've been in the forest," she said, her voice steady. "I felt your presence, felt the change in the air. Tell me, child, what did you see?"

Mira opened her mouth to speak, but the words caught in her throat. How could she explain? How could she tell her grandmother about Kaleb, about the sorcerer with silver eyes who seemed to haunt her every thought? She opened and closed her mouth, her mind still spinning from the night's events.

"Grandmother, I—"

"You met him, didn't you?" Her grandmother's voice was soft but firm, as though she had already known the answer.

Mira froze. "What do you mean?"

Her grandmother's eyes grew darker, and she set the spoon down on the table with a sharp clink. "The Silver-Eyed

Sorcerer," she repeated, her voice low. "He's been waiting for you."

Mira's heart skipped a beat. "What do you know about him?"

Her grandmother stood, her frail form moving with surprising speed as she crossed the room and closed the door to the kitchen. "Sit down, child. There's much I need to tell you."

Mira took a seat at the worn wooden table, her hands shaking as she placed them in her lap. Her grandmother's gaze softened, but there was a weight behind her eyes, something deep and ancient. It was as though she had been expecting this moment, this conversation, for years.

"Kaleb is not just any man," her grandmother began, her voice thick with sorrow. "He is cursed. The curse runs deep, so deep that it has bound him to the forest, to the shadows, to the very magic that keeps him trapped in this realm."

"Cursed?" Mira echoed, her voice barely above a whisper. She felt as if the ground beneath her was slipping away, as if everything she thought she knew about the world was crumbling. "How? Why?"

Her grandmother sighed, her weathered hands trembling slightly as she folded them together. "Long ago, Kaleb was a prince—a ruler of a great kingdom. But his ambition, his thirst for power, led him down a dark path. He made a terrible pact with an ancient sorceress, a being as old as the forest itself. In exchange for ultimate power, Kaleb bound himself to her, to her magic. And in doing so, he cursed not only himself but his entire lineage."

Mira's head spun as her grandmother continued.

"The curse was meant to be broken by a chosen one," she said, her eyes locking with Mira's. "Someone with a pure heart. Someone like you."

Mira's chest tightened. "You mean I—?"

Her grandmother nodded gravely. "You are the one who can break his curse. But you must be careful, Mira. The magic that holds Kaleb is ancient, powerful, and not easily undone. And the deeper you get into this world, the more dangerous it will become."

Mira felt her breath catch in her throat. Kaleb's silver eyes, the power that had surged between them, the creatures in the forest—it was all connected, and she had no idea just how far she had already gone into this darkness.

"And Lyanna?" Mira asked, her voice trembling. "What does she know?"

Her grandmother's expression darkened. "Lyanna is more than just a healer, child. She has her own secrets. She's always known about the curse, and she's been waiting for you, too. But her motives are not as pure as she claims."

Mira leaned back in her chair, trying to process it all. The weight of the truth felt crushing, yet she knew one thing for sure: her life had changed forever. The Silver-Eyed Sorcerer had come into her world, and there was no turning back.

"You must go to him," her grandmother said, her voice soft but filled with urgency. "Before it's too late."

Mira's heart thundered in her chest. "But... how? How can I help him?"

Her grandmother's eyes locked onto hers, filled with a mixture of fear and hope. "The answers lie within him. But be warned, child: the path you walk will not be easy. And the danger you face is greater than you can imagine."

With those words, Mira's world shifted again, this time for good. She wasn't just caught in the web of Kaleb's curse. She was part of it.

Three

A Dangerous Invitation

The rain had begun to fall, light at first, the soft pitter-patter a steady reminder of the world continuing on as it always had. But for Mira, each drop felt like a warning. She stood on the edge of the forest, her heart heavy with questions she couldn't answer. The silver-eyed sorcerer, Kaleb, had been a mystery, and the more she thought about the strange pull between them, the more she realized how little she understood about him—and herself.

The air was thick with the scent of damp earth, and the world around her seemed to close in, the trees bending low as if whispering secrets. Mira pulled her cloak tighter around her shoulders, her eyes scanning the darkened path ahead. There was no turning back now. Kaleb had given her a choice—a choice she couldn't ignore.

A Dance with the Silver-Eyed Sorcerer

His invitation had been delivered the night before, the words written in a language she couldn't decipher, yet somehow, she understood the meaning: Meet me under the full moon. You are the key. The message, cryptic as it was, stirred something inside her—a blend of fear and curiosity, like a flame beckoning her to step closer.

But as she made her way to the clearing where they had last met, the weight of her decision grew heavier with each step. Her grandmother's warnings echoed in her mind: You must be careful, Mira. Kaleb is not what he seems. The forest is full of darkness, and there are forces at play that you cannot yet comprehend. The words were a warning, but they had only deepened the mystery.

Her feet crunched against the wet ground, the noise deafening in the stillness. She wasn't sure what she expected to find, but the haunting quiet of the forest felt suffocating now. The deeper she ventured, the more she felt the presence of something watching her—something ancient and powerful. A shiver ran down her spine as she thought of the shadow creatures that had attacked them, the ones that had been drawn to Kaleb's power. What did he want from her? What was he willing to risk to break the curse?

Suddenly, the soft rustle of movement broke the silence. Mira froze, her breath catching in her throat. She scanned the trees, her heart pounding in her chest. The moonlight filtered through the canopy, casting eerie shadows on the path ahead. Nothing. Just the wind whispering through the branches. But Mira couldn't shake the feeling that she wasn't alone.

A Dangerous Invitation

And then, from the shadows, he emerged.

Kaleb.

His figure was outlined in silver light, the same ethereal glow that had surrounded him the first time they met. His silver eyes caught the moonlight, glowing with an intensity that made Mira's breath hitch. He looked as though he had been waiting for her for an eternity, his gaze piercing through the veil of the forest, and for a moment, Mira forgot to breathe.

"You came," Kaleb said, his voice smooth like silk, but with an edge of something darker. His eyes held a strange gleam—was it relief? Or something else? "I wasn't sure you would."

Mira swallowed, her throat dry. "I didn't have much of a choice, did I?"

A flicker of something crossed his face, but it was gone in an instant, replaced by his usual calm expression. He stepped closer, and Mira took a step back instinctively, her nerves on edge. The distance between them seemed to shrink, as if the very space was charged with an unseen energy.

"You always have a choice, Mira," he said softly, his voice lowering. "But some choices are more dangerous than others."

She felt the weight of his words, as if they carried more meaning than she could comprehend. She didn't know what it was about him—about his presence—that unsettled her so completely. It was as if she were standing on the edge of something vast, something infinite, and if she took one step too far, she would fall into the abyss.

"What do you want from me?" she asked, her voice trembling despite her best efforts to remain calm. "Why am I here?"

Kaleb's lips curled into a faint smile, but it didn't reach his eyes. "You're here because you have the power to help me," he said, his gaze never leaving hers. "And because you are the key to breaking the curse."

The words hung between them, heavy with meaning, yet Mira couldn't understand. What did he mean? She had no power—no special ability. She was just a healer, a girl who had spent her life caring for others. There was nothing extraordinary about her. Nothing that could break a curse.

"You're wrong," she said, her voice tight with uncertainty. "I don't have any power."

Kaleb took another step closer, his presence overwhelming, his scent a strange mix of earth and something darker, something that made her pulse quicken. "You do," he insisted, his voice low and compelling. "You just don't know it yet. You are the one who can undo the magic that binds me."

Mira shook her head, trying to push away the sudden surge of fear rising in her chest. "How?"

"Trust me," he whispered, his silver eyes glinting in the moonlight. "I will show you. But you must be willing to face the darkness."

Mira took a shaky breath, her mind racing. Face the darkness? What did that even mean? There was so much she didn't understand—about him, about the curse, about herself. Yet, despite everything, despite the fear gnawing at her insides, there was a pull, a magnetic force that she couldn't ignore. She felt as though she were standing at the precipice of something far greater than herself, and she was helpless to turn away.

"What if I don't want to?" she asked, her voice barely above a whisper. "What if I'm not ready to face whatever it is you want me to face?"

Kaleb's gaze softened, his expression unreadable. "Then you'll never truly know what you're capable of."

The silence that followed was thick, charged with the unspoken tension between them. Mira could feel the weight of his words pressing down on her, and for a moment, she felt as if she were drowning in them. She had to make a choice—and the longer she hesitated, the more the darkness seemed to close in around them.

"Why me?" she asked, her voice shaking. "Why did you choose me?"

Kaleb's gaze flickered, his lips curving into something that almost resembled a smile. "I didn't choose you. You were always meant to be here."

Before Mira could respond, a loud crack echoed through the trees, followed by the rustle of movement. Kaleb's body tensed, his hand reaching for the dagger at his side. Mira's heart skipped a beat.

"What is it?" she whispered, her voice barely audible.

Kaleb's silver eyes scanned the forest, his senses alert. "Something is coming."

Mira's breath hitched as a dark shape moved in the distance, its form barely visible in the shadows. The ground trembled beneath her feet, and the air grew thick with an unnatural cold. The creatures had returned.

Kaleb's eyes locked onto hers, filled with urgency. "We don't have much time. You have to come with me, now."

Fear gripped Mira's chest, but there was no choice. The creatures were closing in, their snarls growing louder, their forms shifting like wraiths. Kaleb's hand grasped her arm, pulling her toward the trees, away from the clearing. She stumbled behind him, her heart racing in her chest.

As they fled deeper into the forest, the sounds of the creatures grew louder, their pursuit relentless. Kaleb's grip on her tightened, and for a moment, Mira felt as though she might collapse under the weight of it all—the fear, the uncertainty, the power that Kaleb wielded so effortlessly.

And yet, despite everything, a part of her felt a strange sense of belonging. As though she had finally found the place she was always meant to be.

But that sense of comfort was fleeting, replaced by a gnawing sense of dread. Whatever lay ahead—whatever dark secrets Kaleb was hiding—Mira knew one thing for certain:

She was already too deep to turn back.

Four

The Sorcerer's Curse

The moon hung low in the sky, its silver light spilling through the canopy of the ancient forest. The shadows stretched long, twisting unnaturally under the cold gaze of the night. Mira's breath came in shallow, panicked bursts as she tried to keep up with Kaleb's pace. His hand gripped her arm tightly, pulling her through the underbrush with an urgency that sent shivers crawling down her spine.

Behind them, the creatures' growls and snarls echoed through the trees, their pursuit relentless. They were fast—too fast—and Mira could hear their bodies crashing through the foliage, their claws scraping against the earth. Kaleb's silver eyes darted from side to side, his expression hard with concentration as he scanned the darkness for any signs of movement.

"Mira, stay close!" he commanded, his voice harsh, laced with something darker, more dangerous than she had ever heard before.

Mira stumbled but managed to keep pace, her heart pounding in her chest. The forest seemed to press in on her, the trees closing around them like hungry jaws. Every rustle of leaves, every snap of a twig sent her into a heightened state of alert, her senses screaming at her to run faster, but her legs were growing weaker with each step.

The creatures were closer now.

She could feel the dread pooling in her stomach, could hear the deafening sound of their breathing, rough and labored, like some beast hunting in the dark. The atmosphere in the forest had shifted, becoming thicker with each passing moment, as if the very air was charged with an ancient magic. It was as though the forest itself were alive, pulling them deeper into its heart.

Kaleb didn't stop, didn't hesitate. He moved with purpose, his eyes fixed ahead, his jaw clenched tight. It was as though he was running from something far greater than the creatures—something that had been hunting him for much longer than tonight.

"Why are they chasing us?" Mira gasped, trying to catch her breath.

Kaleb didn't answer immediately. Instead, he threw a quick glance over his shoulder, his eyes narrowing as the shadows seemed to close in around them.

"They are bound to me," he said finally, his voice grim. "They are creatures of the curse."

Mira's pulse quickened. The curse. She had heard him mention it before, but now, with the creatures snapping at their heels, the weight of his words took on a more terrifying meaning. Kaleb was no ordinary man, and whatever this curse was, it was not something that could be easily escaped.

"What does that mean?" she demanded, her voice trembling. "Why are they after you?"

He didn't look at her as he spoke, but she could feel his eyes boring into her with a strange intensity. "I was not always this way," he said, his tone almost lost in the wind that howled through the trees. "I was once a prince. A ruler of a kingdom that no longer exists. I made a bargain with an ancient sorceress, one whose magic was stronger than any of us could understand. And in doing so, I bound myself to her—and to the creatures you see tonight."

Mira's heart skipped a beat. The words were so casual, so matter-of-fact, but the implications of them made her blood run cold. Kaleb was a prince. A prince with a cursed past. The shadow creatures, the ones hunting them, were born from this curse—this dark magic that had followed him through time.

"You made a bargain with a sorceress?" Mira whispered, her voice barely audible over the wind. She didn't know why, but her curiosity began to outweigh the fear that had gripped her moments before. There was something about Kaleb that fascinated her, something that made her feel like she was standing on the edge of something she could never fully understand, but was powerless to resist.

Kaleb didn't respond for a long while, the tension in the air growing thick as they continued to flee through the forest. Finally, he stopped, his hand pulling Mira to a halt as they reached a clearing. The trees around them seemed to shift and bend, as though they were closing in, watching.

"This is where it all began," Kaleb said, his voice low, almost reverent.

Mira glanced around the clearing, her eyes drawn to the ground beneath her feet. The soil was dark, almost black, and the earth seemed to pulse with an unnatural energy. It was as though the forest itself had absorbed the power of the curse, and now the very ground they stood on was tainted by it.

Kaleb turned to face her, his expression grim. "The sorceress I bargained with was not of this world," he said, his voice filled with regret. "She was ancient—older than the trees, older than the earth itself. Her magic was bound to the very fabric of reality, and when I made the deal, I thought I could control it. I thought I could use her power to protect my people. To make them immortal."

Mira's chest tightened. "But you were wrong."

Kaleb's silver eyes flickered with something like pain, but he didn't look away. "Yes," he said quietly. "I was wrong. I didn't realize the cost of such a bargain. The magic I unleashed didn't protect my people. It destroyed them. And in doing so, it destroyed me."

Mira's heart twisted in sympathy for him, despite the danger he represented. There was something about his vulnerability, something that made her ache in ways she couldn't explain. He had made a mistake, yes, but it was a mistake borne of desperation. A mistake that had cost him everything.

"The sorceress cursed me to this life," Kaleb continued, his voice raw with emotion. "I became bound to her magic, to her creatures. And now, I am nothing more than a prisoner in this cursed realm. The curse cannot be broken unless someone with pure blood, someone who can withstand the power of the magic, comes to set me free."

Mira swallowed hard, the weight of his words settling over her like a heavy blanket. She could feel the shift in the air—the tension that had built between them growing thick, palpable. There was more he wasn't telling her. She could feel it, deep in her bones.

"Why me?" she asked, her voice a whisper. "Why do you think I can break the curse?"

Kaleb's gaze softened, and for the first time, Mira saw a flicker of something like hope in his eyes. "Because you're the one who was chosen. Not by me, not by anyone—but by the magic itself."

The Sorcerer's Curse

Mira shook her head in disbelief. "I'm just a healer. I don't have any magic."

"You do," Kaleb said softly, stepping closer to her. "You just don't know it yet. It's in you. The blood of the ancients runs through your veins. You are the one who can undo what I've done."

Mira took a step back, her heart racing. The weight of his words threatened to crush her. She was part of this. Part of the curse. And if what Kaleb said was true, she had the power to break it—but at what cost?

Suddenly, a blood-curdling scream echoed through the trees, slicing through the heavy silence like a blade. Mira's stomach turned, and her breath caught in her throat.

The creatures were here.

Kaleb's expression hardened as he reached for her arm, his grip firm and unyielding. "Stay close," he commanded. "They will stop at nothing to destroy us."

Mira's mind raced as the sound of claws scratching against the earth grew louder, closer. The creatures were hunting them, closing in with an insatiable hunger. Kaleb's silver eyes flared, and the air around them crackled with energy. He was preparing to fight, to use the magic that was tied to him, and Mira realized that she was standing at the center of a battle she hadn't asked for—one that would determine not only her fate but Kaleb's as well.

A Dance with the Silver-Eyed Sorcerer

The darkness was closing in. The creatures were coming.

And there was nowhere to run.

Five

A Pact with Darkness

The air had turned still, eerily quiet. The forest, once alive with the sounds of wind and distant rustling, seemed to hold its breath. Mira stood at the edge of the clearing, her pulse racing in her veins. Kaleb's silver eyes gleamed in the dim moonlight, but they were shadowed with a darker intensity than she had ever seen before. He was no longer the enigmatic sorcerer who had saved her once, nor the prince lost to time. Now, he was something else—something untamed, something desperate.

Mira couldn't look away, even though fear gnawed at her insides. The creatures were still out there—she could feel their presence, just beyond the treeline, watching, waiting. But the tension between her and Kaleb was far worse than the looming threat of the beasts.

"I didn't want this," Kaleb said suddenly, his voice low and raw, as if the words were being dragged from him against his will. "None of this was supposed to happen."

Mira swallowed hard. She wanted to speak, to tell him that she didn't understand, but the words caught in her throat. She had no idea what he was talking about—what bargain he had made, what price had been paid. All she knew was that she had come here to help him, to break his curse, but now, standing in the midst of a darkness that seemed to swallow everything around her, she wondered if helping him was even possible.

"We can still leave," she said, her voice shaking as she stepped toward him, desperation lacing her every word. "We can leave the forest, leave the creatures behind."

Kaleb's eyes darkened, the glow dimming slightly, but his expression hardened. "You don't understand, Mira." He took a step forward, closing the distance between them in a way that made her heart race. "There is no leaving. Not for me. And not for you."

A chill ran down her spine. "What are you saying?" she whispered, fear creeping into her voice.

Kaleb's jaw tightened, and for the first time, he seemed to struggle with something—something inside him, something that broke through his usual calm, calculated demeanor. His eyes flickered with something raw, something that Mira couldn't place.

A Pact with Darkness

"I made a pact," he said, his voice barely above a whisper. "A bargain with the sorceress. She gave me power—power beyond anything I could have imagined. But power comes at a price."

Mira felt the ground shift beneath her feet as if the very earth were sinking into an abyss. Power? He had made a deal with a sorceress? Was that what had brought the creatures, the curse, into his life? And now, he was dragging her into it too.

"You've already paid the price," Mira said, her voice cold, almost distant as the reality of his words began to sink in. "Haven't you?"

Kaleb didn't answer, but the look in his eyes spoke volumes. The weight of his past was too heavy for words. Mira could see the toll it had taken on him—the way it had hollowed him out, piece by piece, until only the shadow of the man he had once been remained.

"It wasn't supposed to be like this," Kaleb continued, as if talking to himself. "The sorceress's power was supposed to protect my kingdom. To make it immortal. But when I realized what I had done, when I understood the consequences… I couldn't undo it. Not without a price of my own. And now…" He paused, his voice breaking slightly, "I'm trapped in a cycle. A never-ending cycle of destruction."

Mira's heart ached for him, despite the fear gnawing at her. She couldn't begin to imagine the weight of his curse, the guilt that must have consumed him over the years. But there was something else. Something that lurked behind his words—

something dark and dangerous that she couldn't quite grasp.

She took a tentative step closer, her voice gentle but filled with uncertainty. "You said we could break the curse. That I was the key. What do you mean by that?"

Kaleb's gaze flickered to the shadows at the edge of the clearing, his expression turning hard once again. "It's more complicated than you know," he said, his tone sharper now. "The curse is not just a spell. It's a bond. A bond that ties me to the creatures that hunt me. To the magic that feeds on me. And to the sorceress who cursed me in the first place."

Mira's breath caught in her throat. "You're saying that the creatures aren't just... monsters? They're connected to the curse?"

Kaleb nodded, his face grim. "Yes. They are bound to me, as I am bound to them. When I made the pact, I became their master. And yet, they are my prison. They are the price I must pay for the power I was given."

Mira's stomach twisted in disgust. "So you're telling me they're your responsibility? That you're the one who controls them?"

"No." Kaleb's voice was tight, almost pained. "I don't control them. I never did. The sorceress did. But the curse is a trick—a curse that feeds on power, on life itself. And in return for her power, she took everything from me. My kingdom. My people. My freedom. And now... now I am a prisoner of my own making."

Mira felt her heart break for him, but she also felt a growing sense of unease. Kaleb was speaking of a world of darkness and magic that was foreign to her, a world she hadn't even begun to comprehend. And if she was to break his curse, to save him from whatever fate awaited him, she would need to understand it fully. She would have to make a choice—a choice that might cost her everything.

"And what do you want from me?" she asked, her voice barely above a whisper.

Kaleb's eyes flickered with something unreadable. "I need you to help me break the bond," he said. "The magic that binds me. The magic that keeps the creatures tethered to me."

Mira took a step back, her pulse quickening. "How? How am I supposed to do that? I don't have magic. I'm just a healer."

Kaleb's gaze softened, and for the first time, he looked vulnerable—almost human. "You do have magic, Mira," he said, his voice low and full of meaning. "You just don't know how to use it yet."

The words sent a chill through her. Magic? What was he talking about? Was it possible? And if it was, what kind of power did he believe she possessed?

Before she could respond, a low growl echoed through the trees, shattering the fragile silence between them. Kaleb's body stiffened, his hand instinctively reaching for the dagger at his side.

"They're coming," he muttered under his breath. "They always come when the bond is close to breaking."

Mira's heart raced as she heard the creatures growling, their footsteps pounding through the forest, getting closer by the second. Kaleb didn't seem to notice the growing panic in her chest, his attention entirely focused on the approaching beasts.

"Kaleb—" she started, her voice frantic. But before she could finish, he turned to face her, his silver eyes dark and intense.

"This is it, Mira," he said, his voice low and filled with urgency. "This is where you have to decide. You can leave now. Walk away and forget everything you've seen. Or you can stay and face the darkness with me."

Her heart slammed in her chest, the choice laid out before her with terrifying clarity. She could run, return to the safety of her life before Kaleb, before the curse. Or she could stand by his side, risk everything for the chance to break the curse and free him from the darkness that held him captive.

But something inside her stirred, a pull that she couldn't deny. Despite the fear, despite the uncertainty, she knew there was no turning back. Kaleb needed her. And whether she was ready or not, she was already too deep in this web of magic, darkness, and impossible choices.

"I'm staying," she said, her voice trembling, but filled with resolve.

Kaleb's eyes flickered, a flash of something that almost resembled hope. "Then we face it together."

The creatures were closing in fast. And with that, the pact was sealed.

Six

The Dance of Shadows

The clearing had grown still, as if the forest itself were holding its breath. The low growl of the shadow creatures reached Mira's ears, their presence undeniable, pressing in from all sides. The trees seemed to lean in closer, their branches twisting like gnarled hands reaching for her, the wind rustling the leaves in an eerie chorus. In the midst of this encroaching darkness, Kaleb stood before her, his eyes shimmering with the unnatural light of his curse. The air around them thrummed with tension, thick with the promise of something inevitable.

Mira's heartbeat thundered in her chest. She had made her choice—to stay. To stand by Kaleb's side, no matter what horrors awaited them. But as the creatures drew nearer, as the heavy silence of the forest pressed in on her, she began to wonder if she had made the right decision. Was she truly prepared to face what lay ahead? Was she strong enough to help him break the bond that had cursed him for so long?

Kaleb turned to her, his silver eyes gleaming with determination, yet something else flickered in their depths—a flicker of desperation. His hand reached out, brushing lightly against her arm. Despite the chill in the air, the touch was warm, charged with an energy that Mira could feel right down to her bones.

"You're sure about this?" His voice was barely a whisper, almost drowned out by the rising growls from the creatures surrounding them. "Once we begin, there is no turning back."

Mira swallowed hard, trying to steady her racing pulse. She looked at him, really looked at him—the man who had once been a prince, now bound by a curse that had destroyed everything he once held dear. The weight of the world seemed to rest on his shoulders, but in that moment, it was clear that his fate was intertwined with hers. She could feel it in her chest, a pull so strong that it was as though their very souls were bound together.

"I'm staying," she said, her voice low but resolute. "We'll do this together."

Kaleb's lips parted as though he were about to say something, but then he froze, his eyes flashing to the trees. The creatures were drawing closer now, their growls echoing through the night like the sounds of a coming storm.

Mira's breath hitched in her throat as she heard the creatures' footfalls on the soft earth. They were closing in—fast. And then, as if to answer her growing anxiety, the first of the shadow creatures emerged from the darkness, its glowing red eyes burning through the veil of trees.

Kaleb stepped in front of her, blocking her view of the creature with his tall frame. He stood with an air of determination, a calm that seemed unnatural in the face of the oncoming danger.

"They are not just monsters," he said, his voice low but firm. "They are part of me. Part of this curse. If I cannot break the bond, they will tear me apart."

The creature that had appeared from the shadows growled low in its throat, its body shifting, its form rippling like a shadow caught in the wind. It was massive—far larger than anything Mira had ever imagined. Its claws scraped against the earth, leaving deep gouges in the soil as it crept closer, its eyes never leaving Kaleb.

Mira's heart raced as the creature lunged forward, a blur of darkness and malevolent energy. Without thinking, she reached out instinctively, her hands trembling. Kaleb moved faster, his silver eyes flashing as he raised his hand. A surge of power crackled in the air between them, a burst of energy that sent a shockwave through the ground, sending the creature skidding back, hissing in rage.

The creature recoiled, momentarily stunned by the force of Kaleb's magic, but it recovered quickly, its red eyes burning brighter with renewed fury. It lunged again, faster this time.

The Dance of Shadows

"Mira, stay back!" Kaleb shouted, his voice filled with a warning, but the words barely registered in her mind. The world around her had already begun to shift.

As the creature attacked, Kaleb raised his hand again, a surge of energy flowing through his fingertips, but this time, something inside Mira stirred. The magic she had felt before—the raw, untamed power that had swirled between them—began to rise within her as well. She could feel it, pulsing in her veins, a flickering flame of light that matched Kaleb's dark power. It was as if her very being had been awakened to the magic surrounding them, the ancient forces that bound them both.

She stepped forward, her hands outstretched. The energy that had been dormant inside her flared to life, spilling out of her in a wave of pure magic. The forest around them trembled, the ground shuddering beneath her feet as the air thickened with power. The creature screeched, its massive form contorting as the magic fought against it, pushing it back.

Kaleb's silver eyes widened in surprise, and for the first time, Mira saw something like hope flicker in them.

"You—" He stopped mid-sentence, his voice breathless as he turned to her. "You have it. You have the power."

The realization hit Mira like a thunderclap. It was her magic. The power had always been inside her, buried deep, but now it surged to the surface, answering Kaleb's call, answering the curse that had haunted him for so long.

The creature hissed and lunged once more, but this time, Mira didn't hesitate. She raised her hands, and the magic within her exploded outward, a wave of light and energy that engulfed the creature in its wake. The shadow beast screeched in agony, its form disintegrating into smoke as the magic burned through it like fire through paper. The air around them crackled, the ground beneath their feet shaking with the release of power.

For a moment, everything fell silent. The creatures, the shadows, the danger—all of it seemed to recede into the darkness, as though the very fabric of the forest had been torn open. Kaleb stood still, his silver eyes wide with awe and disbelief.

"You did it," he said, his voice a mix of wonder and something else—something darker, as though the magic they had just unleashed had come at a cost.

Mira's chest rose and fell with shallow breaths as she took in the sight before her—the remnants of the creature, now nothing more than ash in the wind. Her hands trembled from the effort, but the power still lingered inside her, an untamed fire that she could neither control nor fully understand.

"I didn't..." She shook her head, her mind spinning. "I didn't mean to do that. I just—"

Kaleb's gaze locked onto hers, and for a moment, there was no one else in the world. His eyes were no longer filled with the same intensity, but with something far softer—something that mirrored the unease she felt in her chest.

"You have to be careful," he said, his voice low and urgent. "This magic—it's not something to be taken lightly. It's dangerous."

Mira's heart beat faster as the words sank in. She had no idea what she had just unleashed, or what kind of magic lay within her. But there was one thing she knew for certain: the power between them was only growing stronger. The creatures had been banished for now, but the curse was still there, lurking beneath the surface, waiting for its chance to rise again.

Kaleb stepped closer, his hand outstretched. "We've only just begun," he said, his voice steady but filled with an underlying tension. "And this… this is only the first of many tests we will face."

Mira looked up at him, her breath still coming in shallow bursts, the weight of his words sinking in. She had come to help him, to break the curse that had bound him for so long. But now, she realized that breaking the curse would not be as simple as undoing the magic. It would take everything from her—the magic, the heart, and the will to survive.

They were bound together by a darkness that neither of them fully understood, and now, as the shadows began to close in once more, Mira knew that they would have to face it together. Whatever came next, they would have to dance with the darkness—if they wanted to survive.

Seven

The Silver-Eyed Secret

~~~~~

The air in the forest felt thick, as if the very atmosphere were holding its breath. Mira could feel it in her chest—the weight of the magic still humming beneath her skin. She couldn't shake the image of the creature disintegrating before her eyes, or the surge of power that had coursed through her body when she had summoned it. There was something in her now—something that had been awakened, something dark and powerful—and she didn't know how to control it.

She glanced sideways at Kaleb, who walked ahead of her, his posture tense and rigid. His silver eyes flickered with an unreadable expression as he led her deeper into the heart of the forest. The trees here were ancient, their bark gnarled and twisted, their branches stretching high above them, interlacing to form a canopy that blocked out much of the moonlight. The air was heavy with the scent of moss and earth, and the silence felt suffocating.

Kaleb hadn't spoken since they'd left the clearing. His focus seemed solely on the path ahead, his jaw clenched, and his hands balled into fists at his sides. Mira, though, couldn't keep her thoughts from racing. The magic had been too easy. Too powerful. And as it flowed through her, she had felt something else—a strange, almost magnetic pull toward Kaleb, as though their magic were connected, as though their fates were intertwined in ways neither of them understood.

The creatures had retreated, but Kaleb had warned her that their battle was far from over. They were only one small part of something far darker and deeper than either of them realized. Kaleb had made a deal, a pact with an ancient sorceress, but there was so much he hadn't told her. The secrets he kept, the truth he hid behind his silver eyes, gnawed at her with an intensity she couldn't ignore. The more she learned about him, the more she realized how little she truly knew.

"Kaleb," she called, her voice breaking through the silence between them. He didn't turn at first, but she could see his body tense in response, his muscles tightening like a bowstring pulled too far.

He finally stopped and looked back at her, his eyes unreadable. "What is it, Mira?"

There was an edge to his voice, one that suggested he didn't want to talk, that he would rather continue their journey in silence. But Mira had already made her decision. She had stayed by his side, chosen to help him break the curse that haunted him. And if she was going to do that, she needed the truth.

"I can feel it," she said, her voice low but steady. "The magic. The power. It's... inside me. But it's not just mine. It's ours, isn't it?"

Kaleb didn't answer right away. He stared at her, as if weighing her words, and then his lips parted, but he seemed to hesitate. "It's more complicated than that," he said finally. "It's always been complicated."

Mira stepped closer, her heart pounding in her chest. "What are you hiding from me, Kaleb?"

The tension between them grew thicker, crackling in the air like the storm that Mira could sense brewing just beyond the trees. Kaleb's gaze flickered to the shadows, and for a brief moment, Mira saw something—something fleeting in his eyes. It was fear.

"I've told you everything you need to know," he said, his voice low, almost defensive. "Everything you need to break the curse. But there are some things you can't understand, Mira. Some things I can't let you see."

Mira took another step forward, her gaze never leaving his. "Then you're not telling me everything. And if you want my help, I need the truth."

Kaleb's silver eyes darkened, the light within them flickering dangerously. He exhaled sharply, the sound a mixture of frustration and something else—a deep, unspoken sadness that lingered beneath his words.

"The truth is," he said slowly, almost as if the words were being torn from him, "that I was never meant to break this curse. I wasn't meant to be free. And neither were you."

Mira's heart skipped a beat. The way he said it sent a cold shiver down her spine. What did he mean by that? What did Kaleb know that she didn't? She had thought she was helping him, thought she had made the right choice by staying, by trusting him. But now, the more he spoke, the more the pieces of the puzzle refused to fit.

"What do you mean?" she asked, her voice tight with the weight of his words. "What do you mean I wasn't meant to help you?"

Kaleb's jaw clenched, and he turned away, his back to her. He stared into the darkness of the forest, his body stiff, as though the truth weighed heavier than any burden he had ever carried.

"I wasn't the one who was supposed to break the curse," he said finally, his voice hoarse. "It was never meant to be me."

Mira's mind raced, her pulse quickening. She took another step forward, her eyes fixed on his back. "Then who? Who was supposed to break it?"

Kaleb's shoulders stiffened, and for a moment, Mira thought he wasn't going to answer. But then, his voice came, barely a whisper, carried on the wind.

"You were. You were always meant to be the one to free me."

The words hit Mira like a blow to the chest, and for a moment, she couldn't breathe. She took a step back, her legs unsteady beneath her, as though the ground had suddenly shifted, threatening to swallow her whole.

She stared at Kaleb, disbelief etched across her face. "Me?" she whispered. "But I—I'm just a healer. I don't have magic. I don't have what it takes to—"

"You do," Kaleb interrupted, his voice hard and filled with a force that made her freeze. "The magic is in you. It's always been in you. It's in your blood, Mira. The bloodline you carry. The one that was meant to undo the curse."

Mira shook her head, her mind spinning. "I don't understand," she said, her voice cracking. "Why didn't you tell me before? Why didn't you tell me any of this?"

Kaleb turned to face her, his silver eyes filled with something she couldn't quite place. "Because I didn't want you to be a part of this," he said, his voice breaking for the first time. "I didn't want to drag you into my mess, into this endless cycle of power and destruction. But now... now that you've come this far, I can't protect you from it. Not anymore."

Mira's breath came in shallow gasps, the weight of his words sinking into her bones. Everything she thought she knew about her life, about Kaleb, about the magic coursing through her veins—it had all been a lie. She was the key, the one who had been chosen to break the curse, to undo the magic that had bound Kaleb to the darkness. But now, as she stood before him, the truth felt like a heavy burden, one that she wasn't sure she could carry.

"You have to help me," Kaleb continued, his voice desperate now, his eyes pleading. "You are the only one who can stop this. I can't do it on my own. Not anymore."

Mira's chest tightened, her heart aching with the weight of his words. She had come to this place, to this cursed forest, to help him. But now she understood: the curse wasn't just about Kaleb. It was about her too. She was part of this. Part of something much larger, much darker, than either of them could fully understand.

"I'll help you," she said, her voice barely above a whisper, the words heavy with resolve. "But we need to do this together. No more secrets. No more lies."

Kaleb's gaze softened for a moment, a flicker of something like hope crossing his features. But it was quickly replaced by the cold weight of the forest, the oppressive darkness that still lingered all around them.

The silence between them grew long, stretching out as they stood on the edge of something dangerous, something that neither of them could escape.

And as the wind howled through the trees, Mira realized that there was no going back. They were both bound to this fate, to the curse that tied them together—and whatever came next, they would have to face it head-on. Together.

But the shadows were waiting.

And time was running out.

Eight

Unraveling Threads

~~~
~~~

The forest was unnaturally quiet. The air was thick with a foreboding sense, as if the trees themselves were waiting. Mira's boots crunched softly against the moist earth, each step measured, her breath sharp in the crisp air. Kaleb walked ahead of her, his back rigid, the faint glow from his silver eyes cutting through the growing darkness like a beacon.

The moon was hidden behind a thick blanket of clouds, casting everything into an eerie, shadowed silence. Mira could feel the oppressive weight of the forest around her—its secrets whispering in the rustling leaves, its darkness closing in as they made their way deeper. She had felt it before, but this time it was different. It was like the trees themselves were leaning in, as if watching them, waiting.

"I don't like this," Mira muttered, almost to herself. Her words hung in the air, swallowed by the stillness.

Kaleb didn't answer. He couldn't. His jaw was set tight, his focus far away, consumed by something that Mira couldn't grasp. His every movement was deliberate, precise, but his eyes were distant. His gaze flickered to the shadows between the trees, his silver eyes gleaming with a strange intensity.

He had been more silent than usual since they had made their way into the heart of the forest, and Mira had learned not to push him. There were things he kept hidden—things he had yet to tell her. The curse, the bargain with the sorceress, the magic that flowed between them—it was all too tangled, too dangerous for either of them to comprehend fully. But she had promised him that she would stay. She had promised him that she would help him break the curse.

And yet, with each passing moment, the darkness seemed to grow thicker around them. The weight of the unknown pressed on her chest, squeezing tighter with every step.

"What is it?" Mira asked, her voice barely a whisper, though she wasn't sure if she was speaking to Kaleb or to the forest itself. "What are we walking toward?"

Kaleb stopped abruptly, his head turning slowly toward her. His silver eyes gleamed in the dark, an unreadable storm swirling in their depths. He didn't speak immediately. For a long moment, he simply studied her, as if measuring her.

"Tonight, we seek the heart of this curse," he said quietly, his voice so low it was almost lost in the wind. "And there is something you need to know, Mira. Something I've kept from you."

Mira's heart skipped. She stepped closer, her breath quickening. "What is it? What are you not telling me?"

He shook his head, his eyes flickering to the trees again. His expression hardened. "I didn't want to involve you in this. But you're already too deep, and I can't keep you from the truth anymore."

Kaleb took a step forward, his hand brushing against the rough bark of a nearby tree, his fingers lingering there as if the act of touching the forest gave him some sort of grounding.

"The sorceress—she's not just bound to me. She's tied to everything. To the land. To the forest. She has a hold on this place, on me, on my bloodline," he said, his voice barely above a whisper. "And breaking this curse… it's not just about undoing what she's done to me. It's about unraveling her magic from the very fabric of this world. From everything she's touched."

Mira's stomach twisted as her mind processed his words. "Then we—"

Before she could finish, a high-pitched screech shattered the silence, followed by the heavy sound of something crashing through the trees. The ground beneath them seemed to tremble with the force of the noise. Kaleb's eyes flashed with urgency.

A Dance with the Silver-Eyed Sorcerer

"They're here," he hissed, his voice filled with warning.

Mira's heart leaped into her throat as the ground shifted beneath her feet. Something was moving, fast. She could hear the rustling of leaves, the low, guttural growls of something large, something that didn't belong. The creatures—the shadow beasts—they were closing in, and their presence was more oppressive than ever. The trees around them groaned as though reacting to the creatures' approach.

"Kaleb!" Mira's voice was frantic, her body frozen in place.

Kaleb's hand shot out, grabbing her arm with a force that startled her. His grip was cold, the power surging from him like a wave.

"We don't have much time," he said, his voice urgent, desperate. "We have to get to the heart of the curse. We can't let them stop us now."

But Mira could feel the creatures closing in. They were too close. The dark shapes were all around them, moving swiftly through the trees, their eyes glowing like burning embers. Kaleb had been right. These creatures weren't just mindless beasts—they were part of the curse, part of the darkness that had bound him for so long.

And they weren't going to let them escape.

Kaleb's silver eyes flicked toward her, his expression grim. "Mira, whatever happens—"

Before he could finish, the first of the creatures lunged from the shadows, a massive, twisted form with claws that gleamed in the dim light. It was like a living nightmare—a writhing mass of shadow and fury. Kaleb's silver eyes blazed with a fierce, almost savage energy. He raised his hand, and the air crackled with power.

"No," he muttered, his voice low, almost pleading. "Not yet."

But the creature was already upon them. Mira felt the surge of magic, the power swirling around her like a storm, and instinctively, she reached out. A wave of light exploded from her hands, a burst of energy that slammed into the creature with a force that sent it staggering backward. But it wasn't enough. The creature recovered quickly, its glowing eyes fixed on her with an unrelenting hunger.

Kaleb stepped forward, his silver eyes narrowed. "Stay behind me."

He raised his hand again, and the ground beneath them seemed to shake with the power he was unleashing. Dark magic swirled around them, a vortex of energy that pressed against Mira's chest, threatening to choke the breath from her lungs. Kaleb's face was set in concentration, his eyes burning with power. But the creatures were multiplying—more of them emerging from the darkness, closing in.

"Kaleb, we can't—" Mira gasped, her words cut off as she struggled against the pressure of the magic.

Kaleb didn't respond. His focus was entirely on the creatures now, his body trembling with the force of the magic he was controlling. His silver eyes blazed brighter, and the air around them grew heavier, colder.

The creatures howled as they circled them, their red eyes gleaming with malice. Kaleb's power was holding them back, but Mira could feel the strain, the weight of his magic pushing against them. They needed to move—needed to get to the heart of the curse before it was too late.

"I'm not going to make it," Kaleb muttered, his voice filled with an almost bitter realization.

Mira's heart skipped. "What do you mean?"

Kaleb's gaze flickered to hers, the flicker of something ancient and sorrowful in his eyes. "The curse—it's more than just magic. It's in me. In my blood. If we don't destroy the source, it will destroy us."

Mira's breath caught in her throat as understanding dawned.

"The sorceress," she whispered. "She's still controlling you."

Kaleb nodded. "She is. And if we don't undo what I've done—undo the pact—I'm afraid this will never end."

The creatures closed in, their claws scraping against the earth, their growls echoing through the trees. Kaleb's power faltered, just for a moment, and Mira saw the strain in his eyes. They were running out of time.

"We need to go," Kaleb said urgently. "Now."

Mira didn't hesitate. She reached for his hand, her heart pounding as they turned and ran. The creatures followed, their footsteps pounding in the earth behind them. The forest seemed to close in, the darkness pressing in all around them. The weight of the curse, the force of the magic, and the danger of the creatures—everything was collapsing around them.

But they had no choice. They had to find the heart of the curse. They had to unravel it. Before the darkness consumed them both.

And as they ran, Mira knew—there was no turning back now.

Nine

The Silver Blade

The moon had emerged from behind the clouds, casting an eerie silver glow across the forest floor. Mira could feel the change in the air—something had shifted, something dark and ancient that seemed to pulse beneath the earth. She could hear the creatures still following them, their growls reverberating through the trees, but now, their presence felt less immediate, as though something greater was coming.

Kaleb's hand was firm on her arm, pulling her forward through the thick underbrush. His silver eyes darted from side to side, his body coiled with tension, his every movement sharp and urgent. They had been running for what felt like hours, but despite the adrenaline coursing through her veins, Mira could hardly keep up. The magic that had surged through her before—the power that had ripped through the creature earlier—seemed to ebb away, leaving her feeling hollow, drained.

The Silver Blade

"Kaleb," she gasped, her breath ragged. "Where are we going?"

Kaleb's lips were set in a hard line, his focus entirely on the path ahead. He didn't slow down. "We're almost there," he said, his voice low and strained. "I can feel it. The Silver Blade is close."

Mira's heart skipped at the mention of the blade. She had heard the stories—whispers of a powerful artifact that could break the curse. A blade forged from silver, said to hold the essence of a soul, its magic as ancient as the curse itself. Kaleb had told her that only the blade could sever the bond between him and the sorceress, that it was the key to his freedom. But now, with every step they took, the air around them grew colder, more oppressive. The forest seemed to be closing in, its shadows stretching out like twisted fingers, reaching for them, threatening to pull them into the darkness.

She swallowed, forcing herself to keep moving. They were getting closer. She could feel it in the pit of her stomach, a sickening pull toward something she didn't fully understand.

And then, just ahead, she saw it.

A clearing appeared in the distance, bathed in a sickly, pale light. In the center of the clearing stood an altar, ancient and weathered by time, its stone surface etched with runes that seemed to glow faintly in the dark. At the center of the altar, a sword was embedded in the earth, its hilt glowing with an ethereal silver light that sent a shiver down Mira's spine.

The Silver Blade.

Mira's breath caught in her throat as they stepped into the clearing. Kaleb's grip on her arm tightened, and she could feel the power radiating from the blade, the same raw energy that had once surged through her, only now it was colder, darker. Kaleb stepped forward, his eyes fixed on the blade.

"This is it," he said, his voice a hushed whisper. His expression was unreadable, his silver eyes flickering with an emotion that Mira couldn't place—was it fear? Hope? Something more?

He reached for the blade, his hand trembling slightly as he grasped the hilt. For a moment, nothing happened. The air around them seemed to still, the creatures' growls falling silent, as if the forest itself was holding its breath. Then, slowly, Kaleb pulled the blade free from the earth, and as it did, the clearing erupted in a burst of energy. The ground shook violently beneath them, sending Mira stumbling back as the magic from the blade surged outward, crackling in the air like a thunderstorm.

Kaleb's eyes widened in shock as the blade pulsed with an unearthly light, its power overwhelming. Mira's heart raced as the magic seemed to flood the forest, spreading through the trees, into the very soil beneath their feet. She could feel the curse tightening around them, the dark magic that had bound Kaleb for so long surging toward the blade, drawn to it like a magnet.

"Kaleb!" Mira shouted, panic creeping into her voice. "It's too much! You have to stop!"

The Silver Blade

But Kaleb didn't respond. His face was pale, his lips parted as he held the blade aloft, the light from its edge flickering in the dark like a beacon. The energy around them was suffocating, oppressive, and Mira could feel her limbs growing heavy, her breath coming in shallow gasps. She was too close to it, too close to the magic that was spiraling out of control.

The wind howled through the clearing, whipping her hair around her face, and for a moment, everything seemed to go still. The creatures were there, lurking in the shadows, watching, waiting. But now, Mira could feel something else—something far more dangerous. The sorceress. The magic was reaching out, touching her, drawing her into its web.

"Kaleb!" Mira screamed again, but her voice seemed to be swallowed by the storm of magic. She reached for him, but something held her back. A force, cold and heavy, pressed against her chest, making it hard to breathe, hard to think.

Kaleb's silver eyes locked onto hers, his gaze haunted, filled with a pain that tore through her heart. "I'm sorry, Mira," he whispered, his voice shaking. "I can't stop it. The magic—it's too strong. The blade... it's the only way."

Mira's heart skipped a beat as the realization hit her. The blade wasn't just for breaking the curse—it was a sacrifice. The blade had a soul of its own, a soul that would demand payment, and Kaleb's words confirmed it. The cost of the curse, the price of the magic, was more than just his freedom. It was something deeper, something darker.

The clearing seemed to darken further as the magic from the blade began to pulse more erratically. The creatures moved closer, their eyes glowing brighter, their forms growing more tangible. They were closing in on them, hungry for the power the blade was releasing.

"No!" Mira cried, her body trembling as she fought against the weight of the magic pressing down on her. She had to stop this. She had to save Kaleb before it was too late.

The blade's light flickered as Kaleb's grip tightened. He staggered, the energy from the sword surging through him, making his body jerk with each pulse. His breath was ragged, his silver eyes burning with the force of the magic he could no longer control.

"I can't hold it back," Kaleb gasped, his voice thick with pain. "It's too much…"

Mira reached out, her hands trembling as she grasped the edge of the blade. The moment her fingers touched the cold steel, the world seemed to explode around her. The magic surged through her like a flood, her body jerking with the power that now coursed through her veins. She could feel the curse unraveling, the threads of dark magic snapping, but at the same time, she could feel the sorceress's presence, a weight that seemed to choke the life from her.

Kaleb's voice was distant, muffled, as though he were fading. "You're the key, Mira. You have to finish it. Break the bond."

The Silver Blade

Mira's vision blurred as the magic overwhelmed her. Her entire body shook, and she could feel herself slipping, her grip on the blade weakening. The creatures were almost upon them now, their forms fully revealed in the flickering light, their eyes glowing with an insatiable hunger.

With a final surge of strength, Mira pressed her palms against the blade, forcing the magic to bend to her will. The energy around them exploded in a brilliant burst of light, and then—silence.

The world seemed to stop, everything frozen in the moment of release.

Mira's breath was ragged as she collapsed to her knees, her body drained, her vision spinning. Kaleb was beside her, his face pale, his eyes flickering as the last remnants of the blade's magic dissipated into the air.

The creatures were gone. The curse was broken.

But at what cost?

Mira looked at Kaleb, her heart pounding in her chest, the silence pressing in around them like a blanket. The Silver Blade had taken its toll—on them both. And as the clearing returned to stillness, Mira realized that their journey was far from over. They had broken the curse, but the consequences had only just begun.

Ten

Temptation's Edge

Mira's chest rose and fell with each shaky breath, the pounding of her heart a constant reminder that she was still alive. The world around her was quiet now, too quiet. The creatures, the magic, the overwhelming power of the Silver Blade—everything had faded into the stillness of the forest. But that stillness felt wrong. It felt like the calm before a storm, the uneasy silence of a world holding its breath, waiting for something to snap.

She staggered to her feet, her body heavy with exhaustion. Her hands were slick with sweat, her palms still tingling from the residual magic of the blade. She could feel the weight of it deep inside her, a force that was no longer just Kaleb's burden but hers as well. The magic had intertwined their fates, and despite the relief of breaking the curse, she couldn't shake the feeling that something darker was looming just beyond the horizon.

She turned to Kaleb, who was standing a few feet away, his back to her, his silhouette framed by the moonlight that now poured through the trees. His body was still trembling, his silver eyes dull and unfocused, as if the weight of the power they had unleashed had drained him completely.

"Kaleb?" Mira's voice was soft, tentative. "Are you alright?"

He didn't answer right away. Instead, he ran a hand through his dark hair, his face contorting with something that might have been pain—or guilt. When he finally turned to face her, the look in his eyes made her heart sink.

"I'm not sure I am," he said, his voice barely a whisper, like the words were being dragged from him.

Mira took a step toward him, her hand reaching out, but the moment she moved closer, he flinched, stepping back as though she had struck him.

"Mira, you don't understand," he said, his voice tight. "What we've done… it's more than just breaking the curse. The magic—the sorceress's power—it's not gone. It's still here. In me."

Mira stopped, her pulse quickening. She had known this wasn't going to be easy, that breaking the curse wouldn't come without consequences, but hearing Kaleb say it so plainly made her stomach twist. She had thought they were free. She had thought they had done it—freed him from the darkness that had haunted him for so long.

But now, she could see the truth in his eyes. The darkness hadn't just been in him. It had been in everything—woven into the fabric of their world, its influence far-reaching and insidious.

"You're not alone," Mira said quietly, stepping closer, her voice firm with conviction. "We did this together, Kaleb. We broke it together."

Kaleb's gaze flickered to her, but he didn't seem comforted. If anything, his expression hardened, and for a brief, terrifying moment, Mira thought she saw something—something dark—move behind his eyes.

"No," he said, shaking his head. "You don't understand. The sorceress—she was bound to the land. To this place. And now…" He trailed off, his voice thick with something like regret. "Now, I don't know what will happen. The magic I've unleashed… it's not just in me. It's in you, too."

Mira's heart skipped a beat, a cold shiver creeping down her spine. She took a step back, the weight of his words pressing down on her. "What do you mean? I—I'm not like you. I didn't make a deal. I don't have the curse inside me."

Kaleb's silver eyes darkened, his lips curling into something like a bitter smile. "No, you didn't. But you've touched the magic. It's in you now. And whether you like it or not, it's changing you. It's changing both of us."

Mira's mind raced as the realization sank in. The power that had surged through her when she'd touched the blade wasn't just residual. It wasn't just a side effect of their magic. It had marked her. The curse had marked her. And there was no undoing it.

"I don't want this," she said, her voice trembling. "I don't want to be a part of this. I just wanted to help you."

Kaleb's expression softened, but only for a moment. His gaze flickered to the ground, and when he spoke again, his voice was heavy, filled with sorrow.

"I never wanted this for you, Mira. I never wanted you to be part of my curse. But it's too late. We've both crossed the line. The magic is in you, and there's no way to take it back. The question now is..." He paused, his voice low, barely audible. "What are we going to do with it?"

Mira's throat tightened. She knew what he was asking. What they were both asking. The power that had flowed through them—the magic of the sorceress, of the curse—was not just something they could walk away from. It was in their blood now, embedded deep within them. And as much as Mira wanted to ignore it, she couldn't. She could feel it—pulsing, swirling, just beneath the surface of her skin. She could feel it calling to her, whispering promises of power.

The temptation was there. It always had been. Kaleb had felt it, too. They both had, since the moment the curse had first taken root in his soul. Power—magic, dark and dangerous—had always been a part of their lives, whether they'd realized it or not. And now, with the blade's magic still crackling in the air around them, Mira felt it more strongly than ever before.

Kaleb's silver eyes flickered to hers again, and she saw the conflict there. He was struggling, torn between the darkness that had consumed him for so long and the light—the fragile hope—that had emerged when the curse had been broken.

But as she looked at him, Mira realized that this wasn't just about Kaleb anymore. This was about them both. The magic they had unleashed was not going to fade away. It was going to change them, shape them. They could choose to fight it—or they could embrace it.

The silence stretched between them, thick with unspoken words, heavy with the weight of the decision that hung in the air like a suffocating fog. Mira could feel the pull of the magic, the seductive temptation of power that promised freedom from everything that had held her back. She had never been one to crave power, to seek control, but now, standing here, with the blade's energy still sizzling in her veins, she could understand the allure.

"Kaleb," she whispered, her voice shaking. "What if—what if we just let it in?"

Kaleb's face twisted with something like pain, his body trembling as he looked away. "That's the temptation, Mira," he said, his voice rough. "That's the edge. The darkness will always be there, calling to us. It's always been there for me. It will be there for you, too. But once we step over that line, we can't come back."

Mira's heart beat wildly in her chest, her thoughts racing. She could feel the magic pulling at her, feel it wrapping around her like a chain, tightening with each passing second. And in that moment, she realized—she wasn't sure if she was strong enough to resist.

Kaleb was waiting for her answer, his silver eyes searching hers for something—anything—that would tell him what she was going to do.

But the truth was, Mira wasn't sure.

"I don't know," she said softly, her voice breaking. "I don't know if I can fight it anymore."

And there, in the silence that followed, Mira understood the gravity of their situation. The magic, the power, the temptation—it was more than just a test of strength. It was a test of their very souls.

And neither of them knew if they would pass.

Eleven

A Heart Torn Asunder

The night felt colder than it had any right to be. The wind howled through the trees, sending shivers down Mira's spine as she stood beside Kaleb, watching the shadows of the forest close in around them. The moon hung low in the sky, casting everything in a pale, ethereal light that only seemed to deepen the oppressive silence. The forest, once alive with sound and energy, had gone deathly still. And in that stillness, Mira could feel the pull of something dark and dangerous, something she couldn't name but knew was watching them, waiting.

Kaleb had been silent for what felt like hours, his body tense, his eyes flickering with something unreadable. She had never seen him like this—so closed off, so distant. The magic that had once seemed like a spark between them now felt like an anchor, pulling them both into something deeper, something darker.

The power of the curse was still there, still thrumming beneath their feet, beneath their skin. And Mira knew, without a doubt, that they were no longer just fighting the sorceress. They were fighting each other.

"I can feel it," Kaleb said suddenly, his voice so low that it barely carried over the wind. "The magic—it's trying to take hold of us again."

Mira's heart clenched at the sound of his voice, raw and filled with something that sounded almost like fear. She turned to him, her breath catching in her throat. He had always been the one with the answers, the one who knew what to do, how to fight, how to survive. But now, he was lost. He was as much a prisoner to the magic as she was.

"You said we could do this," she whispered, her voice shaking. "You said we could break it."

Kaleb's silver eyes flickered to hers, and for the briefest of moments, she saw something in them—a flicker of the man he had once been, the prince who had been driven by hope, by a desire to protect his people. But that light was quickly smothered by the darkness that had followed him for so long.

"I thought I could," he said, his voice distant. "But I was wrong. The curse… it's not just in me. It's in everything. It's in the very land we walk on. The sorceress's power—it's been woven into the fabric of this world, and no matter what we do, no matter how hard we fight, we can't undo it. Not without—"

His words trailed off, leaving the air heavy with the unspoken. Mira felt a cold pit form in her stomach. She knew what he wasn't saying. She could feel it, too—the weight of the magic, the way it twisted around them, always threatening to pull them under.

"We don't have to give up," Mira said, her voice firmer now, though the uncertainty in her chest gnawed at her. "We can fight it. We've come this far. We can break the curse, together."

Kaleb shook his head, a bitter laugh escaping his lips. "Together. You don't understand, Mira. This isn't just about breaking the curse. It's about what happens after. The price for all of this. The power we've unlocked… it's not just a tool. It's a force. And it has a will of its own."

Mira took a step closer, her heart racing. She reached out, her fingers brushing his arm. "You're scaring me."

Kaleb's eyes flickered to her touch, but he didn't pull away. Instead, he closed his eyes, as though trying to hold himself together, trying to keep the weight of it all from breaking him. "I'm scared, too. But we don't have a choice. You feel it, don't you? The way the magic is clawing at us. It wants to take us. It wants to use us."

Mira nodded, her throat tight. She had felt it, too—the pull of the power, the hunger that had been growing within her since the moment she had touched the blade. The magic had taken root in her, in both of them, and now it was impossible to tell where Kaleb ended and she began. They were bound to the magic, bound to the curse in ways they couldn't escape.

"I can't lose you, Kaleb," Mira whispered, the words slipping from her mouth before she could stop them. She hadn't meant to say it, hadn't meant to feel it, but the truth was there, hanging between them. She had come into this wanting to help, wanting to break the curse, but now, now that they were standing on the precipice, the stakes felt higher than she had ever imagined. The darkness wasn't just something that would destroy Kaleb—it was something that would destroy them both.

Kaleb didn't respond right away. He stood still, his shoulders tight with tension, as though the weight of her words had struck him harder than anything else. When he finally spoke, his voice was a quiet rasp, full of regret.

"I'm sorry, Mira. I never wanted you to be part of this. But you were always meant to be. You were always the key. And now... now I can't protect you from it anymore."

Mira's breath hitched. "You don't need to protect me," she said fiercely, stepping closer, her hand still on his arm. "We're in this together. We always have been."

Kaleb's gaze flickered to hers, his silver eyes dark with something she couldn't understand. For a moment, it seemed like he was about to say something, but the moment was broken by a sudden crash in the underbrush. Mira's heart skipped in her chest as she turned toward the sound.

The creatures. They were back.

A Dance with the Silver-Eyed Sorcerer

Kaleb's hand shot out to grab hers, pulling her toward him. "We need to go. Now."

Mira didn't need to be told twice. She followed him, her heart pounding as they sprinted through the trees. The sound of the creatures' growls echoed through the forest, their movements faster, closer now, as though the magic had roused them from the shadows.

They ran for what felt like an eternity, the night air rushing past them, until they finally broke through the trees and stumbled into a clearing. The ground was uneven, rocky, and the air smelled thick with earth and decay. Kaleb stopped abruptly, pulling Mira to a halt, his breath ragged.

"Mira," he said, his voice low and strained. "This is it. The heart of the curse."

Mira looked around, her eyes scanning the clearing. There, in the center, was a stone altar, ancient and covered in moss, its surface etched with runes that pulsed faintly with dark energy. The power of the curse was palpable in the air, a suffocating presence that pressed down on her chest.

Kaleb's grip on her hand tightened. "This is where it ends, Mira. If we're going to do this, we have to do it now. There's no more time."

Mira's pulse raced as she turned to face him. His silver eyes were filled with something she couldn't place—something torn between fear and resolve.

"I'm with you," she said, her voice steady, though her heart was a storm of uncertainty. "We'll break it, together."

Kaleb's eyes softened, just for a moment, and then the storm returned. He stepped forward, pulling her with him, toward the altar. As they approached, the ground trembled beneath their feet. The runes on the altar glowed brighter, casting eerie shadows across the clearing.

This was it. The final moment. The moment that would decide their fate.

But as Mira stepped forward, she felt something else—a surge of magic, darker and colder than anything she had felt before. It was as though the forest itself had come alive, as though the curse had reached out, its tendrils wrapping around them both.

Kaleb turned to her, his face grim. "You have to be ready, Mira. This is the heart of it. The moment we take this step, there's no turning back."

Mira's heart beat faster as she nodded. She was ready. Or as ready as she could be. Because, in this moment, they were both on the edge of something far greater than either of them understood.

The magic was here. And it was waiting to consume them both.

Twelve

The Betrayal

The forest had fallen silent again, but this time, it was not the oppressive silence of waiting—it was the silence of something stirring. Mira could feel it, a pulse in the air that made the hairs on the back of her neck stand on end. The air around them was thick with dark magic, swirling with intent, as though the very trees had turned against them. Kaleb stood just a few steps ahead, his silver eyes flickering between the altar and the dense shadows that enveloped them. His expression was tense, but there was something else in his gaze now—a weight, a hesitation that hadn't been there before.

Mira's heart raced in her chest as she scanned the clearing. The altar was ancient, covered in twisted roots and creeping ivy, its stone surface marked by strange, glowing runes that pulsed with eerie, violet light. She could feel the power emanating from it, something darker and more ancient than any magic

The Betrayal

she had encountered before. The source of the curse was here, in this place, in the very heart of the forest. And as she stood there, she realized just how far they had come, how far they had fallen into this web of magic and darkness. The price they were about to pay was more than she had anticipated.

"Mira, listen to me," Kaleb said, his voice low, strained, as he turned to face her. His eyes were shadowed with something she couldn't read, something that felt like dread. "Whatever happens next, you have to stay with me. You can't let go of me. Do you understand?"

Her breath caught in her throat, and she took a step forward, her hand reaching for him instinctively. But he held up his hand, stopping her. The tension in his gaze only deepened.

"I mean it," he said, his voice sharp. "The magic here—it's not just about the curse anymore. It's about the pact. About the soul that's bound to this place."

Mira's pulse quickened. "What are you saying?" she asked, her voice trembling despite her attempt to keep it steady. "We can't go back now. We're here to break the curse, to end this."

"I know," Kaleb said, his eyes softening for a moment, though there was something broken behind them. "But there's something I never told you. Something I didn't want you to know."

Mira's heart skipped a beat. "What is it?"

He took a deep breath, his hands trembling as he reached into the folds of his cloak. For a moment, Mira thought he was going to pull out the Silver Blade, the weapon that had caused so much pain. But instead, he produced something smaller—an ancient, worn book, its cover cracked and faded, the pages yellowed with age. He held it out to her, his expression pained.

"This book," Kaleb said quietly, "it's the key to everything. It's the source of the magic that binds me—binds all of us. And it's how the sorceress has kept control for so long."

Mira took the book from his hands, feeling the weight of it in her palms. She flipped it open, but the words were in a language she couldn't understand, written in a script that twisted and spiraled, as if the very text was alive, moving on the page. The air around her thickened, and she felt a strange pull toward the book, an overwhelming need to understand what it contained.

"Kaleb…" she whispered, her voice cracking with the weight of the moment. "Why didn't you tell me this before? Why keep it hidden?"

He looked at her, his expression unreadable. "Because it's not just about breaking the curse," he said softly. "The book—it holds the truth of the pact I made. The truth of what I've sacrificed. What I've lost."

Mira's mind reeled. "What do you mean?"

Kaleb stepped back, his face pale as he glanced at the altar, his voice thick with emotion. "The sorceress didn't just curse me, Mira. She bound my soul to the land—" He cut himself off,

The Betrayal

his eyes narrowing as though the weight of his confession was too much to bear. "But it's more than that. I made a deal with her, and the price was greater than I could ever have known. I sold my soul. Not just mine, but the souls of everyone in my kingdom. The magic… the curse… it's all tied to them. To their souls."

Mira's breath caught in her throat. "No," she whispered, taking a step back. "You didn't—"

"I had no choice," Kaleb's voice cracked as he looked away, guilt and shame mixing in his silver eyes. "She promised me immortality, promised to make my people stronger, but she tricked me. She always had her own plans, her own dark designs. And now, the magic is feeding on me, on my soul. It's in my blood, Mira. It's why the creatures came for me. It's why they won't stop."

Mira could feel the ground shifting beneath her feet, as though the very earth was moving, turning, twisting under the weight of Kaleb's words. The truth of the curse, the depth of the darkness that had been planted in his soul—it was more than she had ever imagined. And yet, the worst part was that it wasn't just his burden anymore. It was hers, too.

"But we're here now," Mira said, her voice trembling with resolve. "We can stop this. We can break it."

Kaleb's eyes flickered to the altar again, and a deep sadness overtook him. "We can try," he said softly, his voice filled with an almost unbearable sorrow. "But it's not that simple. You don't understand, Mira. The pact I made—it's tied to the very fabric of this world. Breaking it won't just free me. It will unravel everything."

Mira stepped closer to him, her hand finding his. "We have to try. We can't just leave it like this. Not after everything we've been through."

He looked down at their hands, his fingers tightening around hers for a brief moment before he pulled away. His face was torn, a war raging behind his eyes.

"The truth is," he said, his voice barely a whisper, "I'm not sure if I can let go of it. The power, the promise of what I could have had—it's still in me. The temptation is too strong, Mira."

Mira's heart pounded in her chest as she realized what he was saying. The temptation was still there, pulsing just beneath the surface. She had seen it in his eyes before—the way the power had lured him in, the way the dark magic had seduced him.

"I don't want to lose you, Kaleb," Mira whispered, her voice breaking. "I don't want to lose you to the darkness."

Kaleb's silver eyes flashed with something dangerous, something raw. He turned to her, his face inches from hers, his breath hot against her skin. "But I don't know if I can stop it," he said, his voice hoarse. "The power—it's in me, Mira. And it's trying to take me."

Suddenly, a sound interrupted them—a low, guttural growl that seemed to vibrate through the ground. Mira's heart skipped in her chest as she looked around, her pulse quickening.

The creatures were here.

But this time, it wasn't just the creatures. The air around them began to tremble with a new energy, a presence that was colder, darker than anything they had faced before. Mira turned back to Kaleb, her heart sinking.

"It's her," Kaleb said, his voice filled with dread. "The sorceress. She's here."

And just like that, the world around them shifted, and Mira realized, with a sinking feeling in her gut, that the final battle had only just begun.

Thirteen

The Heart of the Curse

The clearing was bathed in an eerie, silver light, the air heavy with the scent of damp earth and the unmistakable tang of magic. Mira could feel it pressing against her skin, thick and suffocating. The ground beneath her feet seemed to hum with energy, the ancient runes on the altar pulsing with a low, rhythmic glow. It was as if the very earth was alive, breathing, responding to the magic that had been unleashed.

Beside her, Kaleb stood rigid, his silver eyes scanning the darkness, his breath shallow, as though the weight of everything that had led them here was finally catching up to him. His hands, once so sure, were now clenched at his sides, the tension in his body palpable, radiating from him like an invisible storm.

"They're coming," Kaleb whispered, his voice low, barely audible over the sound of their breathing. "I can feel it."

Mira turned toward him, her heart pounding in her chest. The creatures had retreated when they had first arrived, but now—now, there was something else. A darker presence, a more ancient force that was crawling from the depths of the forest. The sorceress. Mira felt it in her bones—the cold, malevolent pull that had always been there, lurking just beneath the surface.

"The sorceress," Kaleb said, his voice tightening with fear. "She's not just in the forest. She's here—inside the heart of the curse. And she's waiting for us."

Mira swallowed hard, the weight of his words sinking into her. She had known the moment would come—the moment when the final confrontation would unfold. But now that they were standing on the edge of it, she couldn't shake the feeling that they were walking into something far more dangerous than they had ever imagined.

"We have to end it," Mira said, her voice steadier than she felt. She reached for Kaleb's hand, her fingers trembling slightly as she grasped his. "We can break this, Kaleb. Together."

For a brief moment, Kaleb's gaze softened, and a flicker of something like hope passed through his silver eyes. But it was gone almost as quickly as it had appeared. He stepped back, releasing her hand, his face hardening again as the darkness from the trees seemed to gather around them.

"We don't have a choice," he said, his voice low, filled with a resigned bitterness. "But we may not survive it."

Mira's breath hitched as she turned back toward the altar. The runes were pulsing more intensely now, the magic growing stronger with each passing second. The air was thick with tension, charged with an energy that was as old as the earth itself. The curse was alive in this place—alive in them.

And then, the silence was shattered.

A figure stepped into the clearing, emerging from the shadows with an unnatural grace, her presence like a black hole, pulling at the very fabric of reality. Mira's breath caught in her throat as she recognized her.

The sorceress.

She stood tall, draped in robes of midnight black, her skin pale and gleaming under the moonlight. Her eyes, dark as the night itself, locked onto Mira's with a predatory gleam. There was no warmth in her gaze—only cold calculation. Power. It radiated from her like an aura, the very air around her humming with dark energy.

"You've come to finish what you started," the sorceress said, her voice smooth and honeyed, yet filled with an underlying venom. "But you don't understand, do you? This curse was never meant to be broken. It was always meant to bind you—both of you."

Mira took a step forward, her heart hammering in her chest. "We're not afraid of you," she said, her voice trembling but defiant. "We're ending this, tonight."

The sorceress laughed, the sound cold and mirthless, echoing through the clearing like a death knell. "Foolish girl," she hissed. "You think you can break the curse? You think you can undo centuries of magic with a wave of your hand? You don't know the cost of what you're doing. You don't understand the price."

Mira's mind raced as the sorceress's words hung in the air. What price? What did the sorceress mean? She could feel the magic swirling around them, pushing against her, testing her resolve. But she wasn't going to back down—not now. Not when they were so close.

"We understand more than you think," Kaleb spoke suddenly, his voice sharp, cutting through the sorceress's words like a blade. "You made a deal with me, and it's time to pay the price. The curse ends tonight. We're ending it, once and for all."

The sorceress's smile faltered for a moment, her eyes narrowing as she regarded Kaleb. "You think you can destroy me? You think you can erase me from this world? You've always been so blind, Kaleb. So eager to break free of the chains that bind you. But the truth is, you are as much a part of this curse as I am. You always have been."

Mira turned to Kaleb, her heart heavy with the weight of the sorceress's words. "What does she mean, Kaleb?" she asked, her voice barely above a whisper.

Kaleb's gaze flickered to hers, his silver eyes clouded with something she couldn't quite place. He took a deep breath, his chest rising and falling with the weight of the moment. "I made a bargain," he said quietly, his voice low and filled with regret. "A bargain I thought would save my kingdom. I thought it would protect them, make them stronger. But the sorceress's power—her magic—it's always been more than just a curse. It's part of me, Mira. It's been woven into my soul. Into my blood."

Mira's heart skipped in her chest as the realization hit her like a physical blow. "No," she whispered, her voice shaking. "You didn't…"

"I didn't know what I was doing," Kaleb said, his voice thick with guilt. "I didn't understand the price. But I do now. And I can't keep running from it."

The sorceress's laugh echoed through the clearing again, and this time it was filled with something darker, more triumphant. "So, you finally understand," she said, her voice dripping with malice. "The truth is, Kaleb, there is no breaking the curse. Not for you. Not for anyone. It is part of you. It always has been. And now, you'll see that the price is more than just your soul."

Mira turned back to the altar, her mind racing. The air around them crackled with energy, the runes on the stone glowing brighter, pulsing with a fierce, unrelenting power. Kaleb's words—the truth of his bargain, of the sorceress's hold over him—rippled through her like a dark wave. She could feel it now, the weight of the magic, pressing down on them. She could feel the pull of the curse, trying to wrap itself around her, trying to drag her under.

The Heart of the Curse

But she couldn't give in. She couldn't let the darkness win. Not now. Not after everything they had been through.

"We're not giving up," Mira said, her voice firm despite the fear creeping into her chest. She turned to Kaleb, her eyes locked onto his. "We can still do this. We can still end this."

Kaleb met her gaze, his silver eyes dark with uncertainty, but there was something else there, too—something like a spark of hope, a glimmer of something that had been buried beneath the weight of the curse. He nodded, his jaw set in determination.

"Together," he whispered, his voice barely audible.

Mira's heart clenched as she reached for him, their hands meeting in the space between them. The magic surged around them, but this time, it was different. This time, they were ready.

The sorceress's laughter died in her throat as the light from the altar grew brighter, flooding the clearing with an intensity that made Mira's eyes burn. The creatures that had once stalked the forest fell silent, their forms dissolving into the air as though they were nothing more than shadows.

But the sorceress wasn't backing down. She was still there, still fighting, her power swelling, her presence like a suffocating cloud.

And as Mira and Kaleb stood together, facing the heart of the curse, they knew one thing with certainty: the final battle had only just begun.

Fourteen

The Final Dance

The clearing had transformed into something else entirely. The ground beneath Mira's feet was no longer solid, but a shifting mass of power, undulating and alive. The runes on the altar glowed with an intensity that threatened to burn her skin, the air crackling with magic so thick it was nearly suffocating. Every breath Mira took seemed to fill her lungs with the heavy weight of inevitability, each exhale caught in the vortex of energy spiraling around them.

She stood facing Kaleb, her fingers tightly intertwined with his, the pulse of the curse and the magic between them a constant reminder of the darkness they had unleashed. The sorceress was there, too—looming just beyond the altar, her figure both ethereal and terrifying, a shadow that stretched far beyond the physical world. Her eyes, dark and hollow, gleamed with an unearthly power that seemed to reach into the very depths of

The Final Dance

Mira's soul.

"You think you can end this?" The sorceress's voice was a silken thread, wrapped in malice. It slithered through the air like a poison, curling around Mira's mind. "You cannot destroy what you do not fully understand. This curse… it is not just mine. It is yours. You have become a part of it, whether you like it or not."

Mira's breath quickened as the sorceress's words struck her, deeper than she wanted to admit. The weight of everything—the bargain, the magic, the power that had bound them—was suffocating. She could feel the temptation, too, now, the pull of the dark magic that had begun to claim them both. It was stronger than ever, like an invisible hand reaching for her heart.

"Let her go," Kaleb's voice was hoarse, filled with determination and something else—something she couldn't quite place, but it echoed with the same power that had driven him to make the deal with the sorceress in the first place.

The sorceress laughed, the sound echoing through the trees like a cackle from the depths of hell. "Let her go?" She tilted her head, her smile wide and wicked. "She is already lost. As you are, Kaleb. As you have always been."

The words hit Kaleb like a physical blow. He staggered back, his silver eyes flashing with anguish, but his hand tightened around Mira's, pulling her closer to him. She could feel his heartbeat, a frantic pulse beneath his skin, and she knew that he, too, was struggling against the darkness that threatened to overtake him.

"Mira," Kaleb whispered, his voice trembling. "We have to end this. Now."

His words were more than a plea—they were a command, an unspoken understanding between them. The time had come to make the final choice. To step into the heart of the curse and face the truth of everything they had fought for.

Mira nodded, her eyes never leaving his. The forest, the magic, the sorceress—none of it mattered now. Only Kaleb mattered. Only their bond. She could feel the truth settling in her chest, the weight of the power between them becoming unbearable. But she didn't flinch. Instead, she stepped closer to him, her feet moving without thought, drawn by the force of the magic.

"We will face it together," she said, her voice steady despite the turmoil churning inside her. She could feel the magic inside her rising, swirling through her veins like fire. It had always been there—ever since she had touched the Silver Blade. The magic was hers, just as much as it was Kaleb's. And in that moment, as the energy surged through the clearing, Mira knew one thing for certain: they were both going to fight this curse with everything they had.

Kaleb's eyes softened as he looked at her, his hand still gripping hers, the strength in his touch a silent promise. The air around them seemed to hum, a low, vibrating sound that grew louder and louder, until it was almost deafening. The darkness was pushing in, the sorceress's presence creeping closer.

The Final Dance

"Mira, listen to me," Kaleb said, his voice tight with urgency. "The blade, the magic—it's in us now. We have to break it. Or it will consume us."

She didn't hesitate. The blade, the curse, the magic—they were a part of her now, as much as they were a part of Kaleb. She could feel the weight of it pressing down on them, like a thousand invisible hands pulling them toward the center of the storm. But Mira wasn't afraid. Not anymore. She had chosen this path. She had chosen Kaleb. And there was no turning back.

"We will break it," Mira said, her voice fierce, resolute. "Together."

Kaleb nodded, his expression set, and with a final, determined glance toward the sorceress, he stepped forward, leading Mira to the altar. The ground beneath their feet trembled, and the magic seemed to swirl faster, tightening around them as they reached the center of the clearing. The sorceress was waiting, her eyes gleaming with a wicked amusement, as though she knew they had no chance of succeeding.

"You cannot defeat me," she said, her voice dripping with disdain. "I am the source of the curse. The very heart of it. And you, Kaleb, are mine. You always have been. You cannot escape."

Mira's heart raced, but she held Kaleb's gaze, steady and unwavering. She could feel the power rising within her, the surge of magic she had never fully understood until now. It was hers to command, hers to wield, and in this moment, it was the only thing standing between them and the sorceress's grip.

A Dance with the Silver-Eyed Sorcerer

"Kaleb," Mira said, her voice firm. "We can do this."

Kaleb took a deep breath, his fingers tightening around hers. His silver eyes flickered to the sorceress, and for a moment, Mira saw something—something dark and dangerous flash across his face. But then, just as quickly, it was gone. He turned back to her, his gaze softening, and she knew—he was ready.

With a swift motion, he raised his free hand, and the air around them crackled with energy. Mira felt it—the power building, surging through her as if the entire world were holding its breath. The magic was no longer just a tool—it was them. They were the conduit, the key to ending the curse once and for all.

The sorceress screamed, a shrill, guttural sound that tore through the clearing like a blade through flesh. But Mira didn't flinch. She stepped forward, raising her own hand, the magic within her flowing in sync with Kaleb's. Their powers converged, the force of their combined energy bursting outward in a blinding flash of light.

For a moment, everything went white. The world seemed to cease, and Mira felt herself pulled into the heart of the magic. Time stretched and twisted, and she was caught between two worlds—the physical world and the world of magic that lay just beneath it. The curse, the sorceress, Kaleb—all of it swirled together in a chaotic whirlpool of light and shadow, power and destruction.

Then, with a final, deafening crack, the magic exploded outward, sending a shockwave through the clearing. The ground

The Final Dance

shook, the air crackling with energy, and for one heartbeat, Mira thought the world would tear apart. But then, just as suddenly, it stopped.

The clearing was silent once more.

Mira collapsed to her knees, her body trembling with exhaustion. She could still feel the magic, thrumming in her veins, but it was different now. The oppressive weight of the curse had lifted. She looked up at Kaleb, her heart pounding, and saw the same exhaustion in his eyes. But there was something else there now—something she had never seen before. Relief. Freedom.

The sorceress was gone. The curse was broken.

And the final dance was over.

But as Mira and Kaleb sat in the aftermath, the silence was not peaceful. It was the quiet of a battle fought and won, but at a cost. Neither of them knew what the future held. But for the first time in a long while, they were free. Together.

Fifteen

The Price of Freedom

The first light of dawn broke through the canopy, casting pale ribbons of gold across the clearing. The air was still, too still, as if nature itself were waiting, holding its breath for what had just transpired. Mira sat on the ground, her body weary and drained from the battle within and around them. She couldn't recall how long it had been since the curse had broken—time seemed to have lost all meaning in the wake of the magic's release.

Her hands trembled slightly as she lifted them, fingers stained with the remnants of power that still buzzed beneath her skin. The magic woven into the fabric of her being was now an aftertaste, faint but persistent, a reminder of the fight she had chosen. She felt its pull, even now, urging her to embrace it fully. But she wouldn't. She couldn't. Not after everything she had just witnessed.

The Price of Freedom

Kaleb sat beside her, his face pale and his breath shallow, but his eyes were different. The haunted, tortured silver that had once been filled with pain now held a flicker of something new. Hope. Relief. Yet even as he sat there beside her, his silence spoke volumes. There was something still there, something neither of them could put into words.

The price of freedom wasn't something easily understood.

"Kaleb," Mira whispered, her voice breaking the silence that had settled over them. She turned to look at him, her gaze soft with concern, but also with something deeper, something that had formed between them in the chaos of their shared ordeal. "Are you… okay?"

Kaleb's lips twitched, though the smile he gave her didn't quite reach his eyes. He exhaled, a sound of disbelief, of relief, and something else. "I think I'm… free," he said quietly, as if testing the words. "But I don't know what that really means anymore."

Mira nodded, though her own heart clenched with the same uncertainty. They had shattered the chains, broken the bond that had held Kaleb to the sorceress, to the curse. They had succeeded in ending the reign of darkness that had nearly consumed them both. But as the reality of their victory settled in, so did the weight of their actions. Freedom was not a clean slate; it was messy and brutal. They had paid a price—one that neither of them fully understood.

The sorceress was gone. The creatures, the nightmares that had plagued them both, had disappeared with her, leaving only echoes in the trees. But the magic that had once bound Kaleb, that had tied him to the very land, lingered in the air, just beyond reach. There was something unfinished, something unresolved.

Mira stood slowly, her body aching from the strain of the battle. The remnants of the curse still pulsed through the clearing, rippling under the surface of the world, a silent reminder of what had been. She didn't know what would happen to Kaleb now that the sorceress was no more. She didn't know what would happen to them.

She reached her hand out toward the altar, her fingers brushing the stone. The runes had stopped glowing, but the energy in the air still hummed, faint but persistent. She felt the temptation of the power, a part of her that had been awakened and now called to her, urging her to take it all, to use it, to claim it.

But Kaleb's voice, hoarse and filled with an emotion that bordered on fear, broke through her thoughts.

"Don't," he said softly, his voice barely a whisper.

Mira turned toward him, her heart quickening at the look in his eyes. His expression was filled with something—something that was equal parts fear and pleading.

"I can feel it too," he said, his voice tight. "The magic, the power—it's still here. And it's calling to us. To me. To you."

Mira's chest tightened. She knew what he meant. The temptation, the allure of the magic, was undeniable. She had

The Price of Freedom

felt it before—had felt it rising within her when she had touched the Silver Blade. But this was different. It wasn't just the magic she had touched. It was everything. The curse, the sorceress, the power that had been woven into the very land, into her very blood. It was all still there, and it wanted to be used.

But Kaleb was right. If they gave in now, if they succumbed to the power, to the pull, they would lose everything. They would become what the sorceress had always wanted them to be: tools of darkness, pawns in a game much larger than themselves.

Mira swallowed, her throat dry. She could feel the weight of the decision pressing down on her like a suffocating weight. This was the moment that would define them. This was the moment where they had to choose. To fight, to resist, to break free from the chains that had bound them. Or to surrender to the temptation, to embrace the power that had once seemed like a gift but was now a curse in itself.

Kaleb stood slowly, his eyes never leaving hers, his expression unreadable, but there was something there—a shared understanding. They had both felt the same pull. The same hunger for the magic, for the power. And yet, they had come so far to break free of it. Would they let it consume them now?

"I don't know if I can do this," Kaleb said, his voice barely above a whisper, his words trembling in the air between them. "I don't know if I can resist it anymore."

Mira's heart clenched. The battle had never been just against the sorceress, against the curse. It had always been within them.

The temptation. The pull. It was always there, waiting to take them, waiting to drag them down into the depths of darkness.

She stepped forward, her voice steady despite the storm brewing inside her. "Then we'll fight it," she said softly. "We'll fight it together, Kaleb. We've come this far. We've broken the curse. We've freed ourselves. We're not going to let it win."

Kaleb's eyes flickered with something—something that looked like hope, like relief. But there was still uncertainty there, a doubt that lingered in the space between them. He reached out slowly, his hand shaking as he touched her arm.

"I don't know if I can be the man I was," he whispered. "I don't know if I can ever be free of it."

Mira looked up at him, her chest tight, her heart racing. "But we can be something else," she said, her voice low, but filled with conviction. "We can choose to be free. We don't have to be what we were. We can be what we choose to be."

For a long moment, Kaleb didn't speak. He didn't move. It was as though he were weighing her words, testing them against the weight of his own fear and guilt. But then, slowly, his grip on her arm tightened, and a flicker of something warmer, something human, passed through his eyes.

"We'll fight it," he said, his voice steady. "Together."

Mira nodded, her heart swelling with something she couldn't quite name. It was more than just relief. It was the realization that they had made a choice. They had chosen each other. They had chosen freedom.

The world around them was silent again, but this time, the silence was different. It was the silence of peace—of a battle won, not against the curse, but against themselves. The price of freedom was steep, but they had paid it. And now, they stood together, bound not by the magic, but by something far stronger.

Their hearts.

And as the sun rose higher in the sky, breaking the last remnants of the darkness that had once consumed them, Mira and Kaleb knew that the true battle was over. The curse had been broken. The sorceress was gone.

But the real test would be what they did with their newfound freedom. And that, they realized, was a battle they would face together—every step of the way.

www.ingramcontent.com/pod-product-compliance
Lightning Source LLC
LaVergne TN
LVHW020425080526
838202LV00055B/5038